D1461694

The Dog on the Tuckerbox

1926—The first Dog 'monument', hoisted at the nine mile site by an unknown resident.

The Dog on the Tuckerbox

Lyn Scarff

Kangaroo Press

First published in 1994 by Kangaroo Press Pty Ltd
3 Whitehall Road Kenthurst NSW 2156 Australia
PO Box 6125 Dural Delivery Centre NSW 2158
Printed in Hong Kong through Colorcraft Ltd

ISBN 0 86417 627 9

Contents

Foreword

by the Prime Minister,
the Honourable P.J. Keating, MP

Like much of Australia's early folklore, the origins of the Dog on the Tuckerbox are clouded in mystery, uncertainty and controversy.

Yet, as with 'Waltzing Matilda', its origins lie firmly in the Australian bush and the early pioneers—who in this case forged west and south from the colonial headquarters in Sydney, following the explorers searching for the source of the Murrumbidgee River. Numbers of them took up holdings in the district of Gundagai in the period 1830–50.

They were hard and hazardous times with supplies and stores having to be transported along makeshift tracks over rough terrain by bullock teams. To pass the time while often being bogged, or for the river level to fall at crossings such as Muttama Creek near Gundagai, 'bullockies' would recite doggerel and rhymes picked up on their travels—and, sometimes, even write a few lines. Often on such occasions the bullocky's dog would sit guarding its master's tuckerbox and possessions while he was away seeking help.

So was the legend of 'The Dog on the Tuckerbox' born in the 1850s. Whoever the author (using the pen name of 'Bowyang Yorke'), the verse was amended sometime later and promoted as a poem by Jack Moses. Its popularity quickly spread, capturing the imagination of Australians both in the bush and throughout the colony. Though the legend was also immortalised by

Jack O'Hagan in 1937 in his popular song that put Gundagai on the world map, controversy continued over the exact location for the monument—5 or 9 miles from the town—and later, on whether to move the famous monument in, or closer to, the town.

It is perhaps an interesting coincidence that a former occupant of this office, Prime Minister Joe Lyons, had the privilege of dedicating the monument sixty-two years ago—at the 5 mile post outside the town—to the early pioneers.

Lyn Scarff's book is a well-researched, interesting and highly readable account of how a bullocky's simple poem about a dog and a tuckerbox became an intrinsic part of this nation's rich folklore and heritage. It is a story that has surprisingly never been told—and we are indebted to the author whose book admirably remedies that situation. But also more than that—it represents as much a tribute to those early pioneers of this great country as does the monument itself.

P.J.KEATING
PRIME MINISTER

Dedication

When Australia was struggling to determine its national identity, it was always to the bush that we looked when comparing ourselves with other cultures.

The pure Australian accomplishments and activities of gold mining, droving, cattle raising, shearing, bullock-driving and bushranging took place in the outback—the vast Australian interior—and were perceived as the authentic life of a true Australian.

These powerful images of the bush circulate in song, story and film, touching the hearts of Australians.

Still, we often forget what it took to settle this land, as evidenced by the stirring speech by Dad Rudd, MP, in the 1940 movie of the same name in which he reminds the parliament of our origins.

Some people have complained about the cost of raising this dam another 50 feet. I want them to think of the people who made this work necessary. The pioneers who crossed the plains in their dragging, creaking drays, strode through the silence of the bush and made it ours. Many of their names are not engraved on tablet or tombstone, and they have no place in the history of our country so far as it is yet written.

But they are the men and women who gave our country birth.

The Dog on the Tuckerbox Monument was dedicated in 1932 to those pioneers. It was the first such monument to be so dedicated. This book traces the events, the people and the controversies surrounding this celebrated monument.

Lachlan Macquarie, governor of New South Wales from 1810 to 1821, is credited with the erection of the first milestones in New South Wales. These milestones and other public works were to him an avowal of his private belief that 'the colony was the beginning of a new corner of Empire'.

Two milestones, the nine and the five, on the Sydney road northeast of Gundagai, which were installed many years after Macquarie's term of office, became the centre of a huge argument which for some years split the town of Gundagai into the 'nine-milers' and the 'five-milers'. Although the argument has quietened down today, there is still confusion surrounding the issue, which emanated from a simple poem written by a bullocky about a dog and his tuckerbox.

A young descendant of Gundagai pioneers, Hayley Nicholls joined thousands of celebrants to share the Dog's 60th anniversary.

Introduction

The now defunct newspaper *Smith's Weekly* carried an article in its 31 July 1937 edition entitled 'Gundagai's Dog Is Gilt-Edged Investment—How Digger's Brain-Wave Saved Hospital'.

Its introductory paragraphs read:

> Motorists who traverse the Hume Highway between Sydney and Melbourne, generally feel interest in the statue of the Dog On the Tucker Box, which has been erected beside Sugar O'Brien's Creek, five miles on the Sydney side of Gundagai.
>
> Most of them feel sentimental over the old pioneers and the bush poet who immortalised the dog; some even stop the car and read the inscriptions.
>
> But there are few who know that that dog stood between the Gundagai Hospital and serious financial embarrassment and that today it represents a sound investment which returns an annual income to the funds of the institution. Gundagai has capitalised on its dog.

The writer goes on to outline what happened from the writing of the original dog on the tuckerbox doggerel in the mid-1850s to the launching of the monument by the prime minister in 1932.

It is one of the most thorough articles written on the Dog that I have seen, but it goes nowhere near revealing the controversies surrounding it. No newspaper or magazine article could.

No attempt is made to introduce the nine-mile/five-mile conundrum; why do the poem and the original recordings of the song say 'Nine miles from Gundagai'? Instead the writer has accepted that the original poem and doggerel had 'five' miles in their text.

Nor did the article discuss whether the dog 'shat' or 'sat' on or in the tuckerbox.

However, to fill you in, the article continued:

> Away back in 1859, a bush versifier who used the pen-name of 'Bowyang Yorke', wrote a set of rhymes which were printed in the local newspaper. The verses, if such they can be called, were quite without merit. As long as the poet could find two words of similar vowel sound, he finished the lines with them and filled in the blanks with any old words.

But the Muse was lurking about somewhere and a stray shot from her quiver hit its mark. The poet concluded the set with two lines which stuck in everybody's memory:

> The dog sat on the tucker-box
> Five miles from Gundagai.

More than half a century passed. A writer who did possess a sense of music and rhythm, Jack Moses, felt that these two lines were deserving of a better setting. He used them for his finale, but wrote a real bush rhyme to act as their escort. He restored the apparently dead; the dog came to life and all Australia knew him and loved him and metaphorically patted his head. Gundagai was placed once more on the map.

A little later, the Gundagai Hospital got into low water, after the manner of hospitals generally. The local board was at its wits' ends to raise money to get it out of debt—a debt of £2000 which seemed impossible of liquidation. But the board was fortunate in having among its members Mr O.A. Collins, a man who had followed his experiences in the AIF by touring the world and—what is far more important—noticing what methods of other nations might be profitably utilised in Australia.

I got the idea of boosting that dog in good American

fashion. I thought out a dozen ways and finally decided on the statue. Then I had to persuade the rest of the board to take a risk. At first, they didn't like the idea of adding more to a debt they weren't able to pay; but at last, I convinced them and contrived to get £75 to gamble with.

Then we had to work out a plan to get publicity for the dog and the unveiling ceremony—for that was to be the moneymaker. There was a Back To Gundagai Week just about due, and I persuaded the people in charge to join forces with me. We did the same with a local annual railway picnic. Then we wrote to the Prime Minister to help us out. Joe Lyons agreed to carry out the unveiling ceremony, and when that was fixed, we got busy with the Press—all brands of it—and the radio people and they both stood by us splendidly.

Our programme carried a week of festivities, races, a ball, gathering of pioneers, and the rest of it. The great day being the Monday when the statue was to be unveiled as a memorial to the pioneers by the Prime Minister, as the climax to the procession headed by Granny Luff, the grand old woman of the district, who was then 90 years of age.

I was always optimistic, but none of us had the slightest idea it would turn out such a winner. We raised sufficient money that week to pay off the £2000 debt on the hospital and when we had collected the government pound for pound subsidy we were £1000 in credit. The town was eaten bare and quaffed dry before Monday. We had to send trucks to towns miles away for more food and drink.

But that wasn't all of it. I realised that we could go on raking off the profits of that dog to eternity. I got the hospital to copyright the photos of the monument and collect 20 per cent of the sales of all the souvenir stuff. We started on picture-postcards. Then we got out silver dog-spoons, dog-folders, and dog-cups and saucers and plates. There's not a day passes now without some motorist going through buying the mementoes.

A Yank told me that Gundagai was the only live town he had butted into in Australia. No wonder we feel inclined to pat that dog on the head every time we pass.

The Dog as it stands today, in front of the shop and kiosk, set in bush surroundings, with picnic and barbecue facilities.

1 How Gundagai Began

As far as size, wealth, glittering splendour or scenic grandeur is concerned, very few indeed of the western towns of New South Wales would be worthy of more than passing note, but their history is rich in the traditions of the past and must be linked forever with those intrepid explorers who illuminated the dark interior of a vast new continent, and with the stalwart pioneers who pushed out beyond 'the limits of settlement' to establish precarious holdings 'far from the haunts of man' ... unafraid of the vagaries of nature or natives, these dauntless settlers laid the foundations of the settlements that today constitute the towns of New South Wales's famed pastoral interior.

A. Gaunt, *A History of Gundagai*

Gundagai is one of those towns. It was established on the banks of the Murrumbidgee River because it was a favourable crossing place. From 1858, when Captain Francis Cadell navigated the Murrumbidgee and arrived in Gundagai, the town received an advantage over all inland towns as an important place of commerce that it could not have derived from any other source.

Practically all the country now occupied by New South Wales, Victoria, South Australia, the Northern Territory and Queensland formed one province. At that time settlement was confined to the east coast for about 200 kilometres (120 miles) north and south of Sydney, but extended inland to Bathurst and Goulburn from which Gundagai is 217 kilometres (130 miles) farther west.

Following the crossing of the Blue Mountains in 1813, many of the more adventurous of the free settlers quickly settled the lands west and southwest of the mountains.

A vast new continent lay open, and Gundagai's first years were connected with three of the most famous inland explorations in the annals of early Australian history.

In 1824, Hamilton Hume was requested by Governor Sir Thomas Brisbane to form an expedition to the shores of Western Port, at the same time reporting on the nature of the intervening country. Accompanied by Captain Hovell, he crossed the Murrumbidgee River at Jugiong, 40 kilometres (24 miles) from Gundagai.

Immediately following this journey, the first settlers followed Hume's track and took up holdings in the district of Gundagai.

In his journey to trace the Murrumbidgee to its source, Captain Charles Sturt reached Jugiong in November 1829. After leaving the most westerly homestead, the party crossed that river on 28 November at a spot where some stockmen had effected a passage, and where Gundagai now stands.

Major Thomas Mitchell published his favourable report following his journey of 1836, and settlers followed explorers, to take up holdings even though they were 'beyond the limits of settlement'.

Gundagai was first called The Crossing. The Murrumbidgee River at Gundagai was nowhere near a problem to cross as was the Mutta Muttama Creek at Coolac, which is a village about nine miles from Gundagai. Pioneers have recorded in diaries and letters that they became bogged in an unnamed place prior to reaching Gundagai. This was almost certainly in the region of Coolac, which was an area of swamp and bad drainage.

2 Bullocky Bill

Poor bullocky Bill! In the circles select of the scholars he hasn't a place. But he walks like a man, with his forehead erect, and looks at God's day in the face.

Town & Country Journal, 1876

When Henry Lawson met a bullocky he had known in his youth, he wrote:

I remembered him when the bullock drivers camped at our place long ago, as being small, nuggety and sandy, and vaguely blasphemous; and wearing elastic sided boots (or larstins), a black suit, a wire-rimmed hat, and a white shirt (biled rag), sometimes pleated.

We talked of the old days and the droving days and the digging days. I saw the glaring white roads, and the dust, and the teams toiling on, or the teams bogged, and all the cruelty that was there. Or, as a relief, camped, with tarpaulins down all round the wheels, in the tall, rain-darkened stringybarks, and the ground steaming round the great fire.

The First Fleet introduced bullocks to Australia in 1788, bought at the Cape of Good Hope. During the second year of settlement, when the colony was desperate for food, most of the cattle which had not died of disease were killed for rations.

The remainder, four cows and two bulls, escaped into the bush. According to L. Braden in *Bullockies,* although it seemed a tragedy at the time, it proved a blessing in disguise. Seven years later the cattle reappeared, wandering along the Hawkesbury River at Cowpastures—a fine herd of 60 cattle was discovered by convicts who had been given grants of land.

Bullocks began to play an important part in the settlement of Australia, first for ploughing, but later as beasts of burden. Hume and Hovell used them in their 1824 expedition, and Captain Sturt took eight pack bullocks. The early settlers literally could not have existed without them.

Soon bullocks, the men who drove them and their dogs which kept them in line were hauling wool, wood, mining equipment, even moving houses, and bringing in supplies of food to remote regions, under conditions that required the use of toughness and ingenuity to get the job done.

Bullock teams have also been used to plough up roads, tow an ambulance which had dropped a wheel into a large rut on a country track, and tow a hearse to the cemetery. In so doing the teamsters established and maintained a 'unique Australian accomplishment—bullock driving', as *The Colonist* of 1867 generously described it.

Called a 'bullocky', and often nicknamed Bullocky Bill, but nearly always having 'bullocky' as a prefix to their first name, these men were popularly supposed to consist principally of boots, beard and blasphemy, the latter unquestionably brought on by the trying conditions.

The *Australian National Dictionary* quotes the *Sydney Truth* of 1901: 'You have no estimation of the great Australian nation till you listen to a bullock driver swear.'

No one can say precisely what happened to inspire the doggerel of the bullocky and his dog near Gundagai, nor can they say that anything happened at all. There were bullockies and their teams and their dogs, and their tuckerboxes. They got bogged at times, and had to wait out flooding of the creek at times.

At all camping spots, and there were very many, they would have spent their nights yarning and bringing news of other districts. If a hotel were nearby and had a piano, there was singing and recitations of the poems the bullockies loved to make up.

AN OLD MASTER by C.J. Dennis

We were cartin' laths and palin's from the slopes of
Mount St Leonard,
With our axles near the road-bed and the mud as stiff as
glue;
And our bullocks weren't precisely what you'd call
conditioned nicely,
And meself and Messmate Mitchell had our doubts of
gettin' through.

It had rained a tidy skyful in the week before we started,
But our tucker-bag depended on the sellin' of our load;
So we punched 'em on by inches, liftin' 'em across the
pinches,
Till we struck the final section of the worst part of the
road.

We were just congratulatin' one another on the goin',
When we blundered in a pot-hole right within the sight
of goal,
Where the bush-track joins the metal. Mitchell, as he
saw her settle,
Justified his reputation at the peril of his soul.

We were in a glue-pot, certain—red and stiff and most
tenacious;
Over naves and over axles—waggon sittin' on the road.
"Struth' says I, 'they'll never lift her. Take a shot from
Hell to shift her.
Nothin' left but to unyoke 'em and sling off the blessed
load.'

Now, beside our scene of trouble stood a little one-
roomed humpy,
Home of an enfeebled party by the name of Dad McGee.
Daddy was, I pause to mention, livin' on an old-age
pension
Since he gave up bullock-punchin' at the age of eighty-three.

Startled by our exclamations, Daddy hobbled from the shanty,
Gazin' where the stranded waggon looked like some half-
foundered ship.
When the state o' things he spotted, 'Looks,' he says,
'like you was potted',
And he toddles up to Mitchell. 'Here,' says he, 'gimme
that whip.'

Well! I've heard of transformations; heard of fellers sort
of changin'
In the face of sudden danger or some great emergency;
Heard the like in song and story and in bush traditions hoary,
But I nearly dropped me bundle as I looked at Dad McGee.

While we gazed he seemed to toughen; as his fingers
gripped the handle
His old form grew straight and supple, and a light leapt
in his eye;
And he stepped around the waggon, not with footsteps
weak and laggin',
But with firm, determined bearin', as he flung the whip
on high.

Now he swung the leaders over, while the whip-lash
snarled and volleyed;
And they answered like one bullock, strainin' to each
crack and clout;
But he kept his cursin' under till old Brindle made a
blunder;
Then I thought all Hell had hit me, and the master
opened out.

And the language! Oh, the language! Seemed to me I
must be dreamin';
While the wondrous words and phrases only genius could
produce
Roared and rumbled, fast and faster, in the throat of
that Old Master—
Oaths and curses tipped with lightning, cracklin' flames
of fierce abuse.

Then we knew the man before us was a Master of our callin';
One of those great lords of language gone for ever from Outback;
Heroes of an ancient order; men who punched across the border;
Vanished giants of the sixties; puncher-princes of the track.

Now we heard the timbers strainin', heard the waggon's loud complainin',
And the master cried triumphant, as he swung 'em into line,
As they put their shoulders to it, lifted her, and pulled her through it:
'That's the way we useter do it in the days o' sixty-nine!'

Near the foot of Mount St Leonard lives an old, enfeebled party
Who retired from bullock-punchin' at the age of eighty-three.
If you see him folk will mention, merely, that he draws the pension;
But to us he looms a Master—Prince of Punchers, Dad McGee!

Bullock teams crossing the Murrumbidgee in 1861 at the southern end of Homer Street, North Gundagai. (Courtesy National Library, Canberra)

Like all early Australians, the bullockies were a cross-section of educated, talented, uneducated and illiterate men. But it is their reputation for a certain crudeness of language which has brought about the controversy regarding what the dog did on or in the tuckerbox.

It offends most people to think that a dog could have soiled foodstuffs in his master's tuckerbox, which, anyway, would at nearly all times have been closed when his master was not nearby.

Yet it is that very incongruity which would have appealed to a bullocky's sense of outrage. What worse could happen to a hardworking honest true-blue bloke after being bogged and having a bullock break his yoke, than to have his dog, his best mate, sit in his tuckerbox, or even flagrantly use it as a toilet!

Over many years the Dog has inspired poems, many of which got their run in the local Gundagai newspaper. One has contributed to the story that the dog sat waiting forever and a day on his tuckerbox for his master to return.

But there are two reports of the origins of the doggerel and where it was written which carry the most weight. Neither is completely accurate in its content, and together they embody the essential characteristics of the controversy surrounding the Dog's history.

One comes from Cyril Sullivan, a farmer and the storekeeper at Coolac (which is nine miles from Gundagai), who died in 1976 at the age of 82. Over the years he vehemently maintained that his father had met the bullocky who wrote the verses, and the site where the bullocky was camped was nine miles from Gundagai.

The other version is recorded in Gaunt's *History of Gundagai*.

In a letter to the *Gundagai Independent* in 1976, when the old nine mile/five mile argument flared up again due to the initiation of a 'referendum' to consider moving the Dog into the town of Gundagai, Cyril Sullivan wrote:

Dear Sir,—Jack Moses did not write the original verse (poem if you like) of the Dog On The Tuckerbox. It was written by the bullock driver when he was bogged at the Nine Mile.

Other than Charlie, no one knew his name, but he was an educated man my father told me.

One wet afternoon, when I was staying at Ushers [Sydney hotel], Jack Moses, Stanley Mackay and a lady called.

We yarned for over two hours and of course the 'poem' was discussed. He did not write it, but said he altered several words in it and sent a 'clean' copy to three places—the Mitchell Library, the Herald and Telegraph libraries.

I heard the original verse twice. Once from my father, who warned me never to ask him again as he would never repeat it.

This was about 1906–7. My father died in 1915. Also once recited, with relish, by Tom Collins at a party.

I am sick of hearing and reading the lies about the Five Mile.

(Tom Collins was a Member of the Legislative Assembly at the time of the dog monument launch.)

Sullivan's story was backed up by a letter published in 1986 by Anne Wakem of Coolac, which said:

As I have always been interested in the history of our area, I would like to share with you, and your readers some information given to me many years ago by Mr Cyril Sullivan of 'Stonehurst', Coolac.

The story of Bill the Bullocky and his being bogged in the Five or Nine Mile Creek.

Mr Sullivan told me that his father had bullock teams (there was a photo of one of his bullock teams at his property, Stonehurst), and quite often he told me that his father would have to take his bullock team down behind the old inn at the Nine Mile Creek crossing of the Muttama Creek to extract stranded bullock waggons.

Years ago the main road didn't run on the route it takes today and this spot was the common crossing place.

The old inn stands as the residence of the Cotterill family. Local people would know how deep and wide the Muttama Creek gets quite regularly in the winter and spring.

In my mind I can see the stranded bullock teams on the wrong side of the Muttama Creek waiting for the water level to drop so they could deliver their supplies to Gundagai.

Charles McAlister, (bullocky and author) and no doubt any other teamsters would have cursed that creek crossing and their experiences would have been the basis of the 'Bill the Bullocky' legend.

No doubt many teamsters would have tried to cross the muddy Muttama Creek before the banks had sufficiently hardened enough to take the weight of a laden bullock dray.

So in conclusion I can only believe my old friend, Mr Cyril Sullivan, and say to you—'And the Dog sat on the Tuckerbox Nine Miles from Gundagai'. Anne Wakem, Coolac.

Apart from these two testimonials, we know the original doggerel and poem contained the words 'nine miles', because Jack Moses used the doggerel's tag lines, 'And the dog sat on the tuckerbox nine miles from Gundagai' for his poem.

He had first become familiar with the fame of the Dog while visiting the Gundagai Show in the 1880s, in his capacity as a wine salesman.

Some unknown thinker who belonged to the show's organisation exhibited a replica of a dog on a tuckerbox in a conspicuous position. Moses saw it, and fascinated as he was with bush lore, remembered it. At the same time, no doubt during his convivialities with the locals, he was introduced to the original doggerel.

It has been consistently said and written that a copy of the original doggerel had been taken from the *Gundagai Times* office.

It was stuck on cardboard and hung on the door of the Royal Hotel, Gundagai, which the following article in a Sydney paper in the late 1930s confirms.

Yesterday afternoon in a general knowledge test conducted by the Australian Broadcasting Commission, someone was asked 'Who wrote "The Dog Sat on the Tuckerbox Nine Miles from Gundagai?"'. The answer was 'Mr Jack Moses'.

Mr Frank Clune, author, denied that that was correct. He said he and Mrs Clune had been told in Gundagai that Mr Moses had not written the poem, and that Mr Moses had copied it 50 years ago, from a poem stuck on the back of a door in a pub in Gundagai.

(Jack Moses has been unfairly judged here. He did after all, write a poem called 'Nine Miles from Gundagai', which poem was the one used to gain publicity for Gundagai by the entrepreneurial newsagents Collins and O'Sullivan. He has always admitted there was a crude version of doggerel around before he wrote his poem.)

More of the Nine Mile version later.

For the version that the doggerel was written at the five mile site, we must go to A. Gaunt's *History of Gundagai* which he wrote as a thesis in 1944 while a teacher at the Gundagai public school.

(Mr Gaunt had the advantage of a lot of data, which he refers to in his thesis as Appendix A. However, when his work was transformed into a book in 1979 no sign could be found of Appendix A.)

Declaring that he had gone to some length to get the story correct, Mr Gaunt says:

In the year 1858, a bullock driver whose actual name has been forgotten, but who was alluded to as Bullocky Bill, was bringing a load of groceries and rum to one of the hotels at Gundagai. On arrival, it was found that the rum had been broached, and the hotel refused to take delivery. The incident became a popular joke with bullock drivers, and Gundagai soon became well known as the drivers spread the tale far and wide.

But that was not all. Early in the following year the same bullock driver became bogged at the Five Mile Creek (known then as Splitter's Creek). After fruitless attempts to extract his waggon, he gave up, and went to have lunch and found his dog sitting? in the tuckerbox.

Coming so soon after the previous episode, the joke was a great one among bullock drivers, and one of them quickly composed a rhyme which soon after appeared in the *Gundagai Times* of June 20, 1859.

It must be remembered that Gaunt, not a native of Gundagai, would have been influenced by the site of the monument which is at the Five Mile flat.

The facts may well be accurate as to how it came about that the doggerel was written. I didn't see, hear or read any other version. It's not improbable. But a similar story was printed in the *Gundagai Independent* in their souvenir edition of 1 December 1932, so Gaunt could merely have copied it from that. And there are similar stories of the bullock drivers' habit of tampering with consignments of spirits, and their devious attempts to hide their thefts.

But to utterly confound matters, the doggerel can't be located. It wasn't printed in the *Gundagai Times* because that paper didn't start until 1868. The *Times* was preceded by the *Adelong Mining Journal and Tumut Express*, and the *Wynyard Times*, both also started by *Times* founder, J.B. Elworthy.

The relevant paper has to be the once-a-week *Adelong Mining Journal* which ran from 1858 to 1860 and was widely distributed in Gundagai. The *Journal*'s copies in the National and Mitchell Libraries are not complete.

I have gone through each available copy of the *Journal*, and although it did feature a poem in each issue, I did not set eyes on the Dog doggerel.

But most importantly, 20 June 1859 was a Monday, and not one of the newspapers came out on a Monday. That date appears to have been either fabricated or misprinted, and the error perpetuated over the years.

According to older Gundagai residents though, the issue carrying the doggerel was still at the *Times*' premises in 1932.

The following doggerel is accepted as being the original. There are other versions, where the opening lines are 'As I was coming down Talbingo Hill', and 'I'm used to punchin' bullock teams'.

By Charlie 'Bowyang' Yorke? A. Gaunt used this name in his History.

> As I was coming down Conroy's Gap,
> I heard a maiden cry;
> 'There goes Bill the Bullocky,
> He's bound for Gundagai.
> A better poor old (beggar)
> Never earnt an honest crust,
> A better poor old (beggar)
> Never drug a whip through dust.'
> His team got bogged at the nine mile creek,
> Bill lashed and swore and cried:
> 'If Nobby don't get me out of this,
> I'll tattoo his (bloody) hide.'
> But Nobby strained and broke the yoke,
> And poked out the leader's eye;
> Then the dog sat on the Tucker Box
> Nine miles from Gundagai.

(The words in brackets were said to have been blanked out when the verse was printed in the newspaper.)

NINE MILES FROM GUNDAGAI by Jack Moses

> I've done my share of shearing sheep,
> Of droving and all that;
> And bogged a bullock team as well,
> On a Murrumbidgee flat.
> I've seen the bullock stretch and strain
> And blink his bleary eye,
> And the dog sit on the tuckerbox
> Nine miles from Gundagai.
>
> I've been jilted, jarred, and crossed in love,
> And sand-bagged in the dark,
> Till if a mountain fell on me,
> I'd treat it as a lark.

It's when you've got your bullocks bogged,
That's the time you flog and cry,
And the dog sits on the tuckerbox
Nine miles from Gundagai.

We've all got our little troubles,
In life's hard, thorny way.
Some strike them in a motor car
And others in a dray.
But when your dog and bullocks strike,
It ain't no apple pie,
And the dog sat on the tuckerbox
Nine miles from Gundagai.

But that's all past and dead and gone,
And I've sold the team for meat,
And perhaps, some day where I was bogged,
There'll be an asphalt street.
The dog, ah! well he got a bait,
And thought he'd like to die,
So I buried him in the tuckerbox,
Nine miles from Gundagai.

3 Where Was the Doggerel Written?

Something yet of doubt remains,
Which only thy solution can resolve.

Milton

There is no doubt that teamsters camped at both the five mile and the nine mile sites, as they did at many spots on their long, slow journeys, and it was customary to identify the camping sites in relation to their distance from a town or village. There was only one regular crossing place, however, and that was in the vicinity of the old Coolac Hotel, about nine miles from Gundagai.

The Coolac Hotel was also used as a post office in those days, and would have been a more popular camping site for that reason.

The Southern Road at that time ran on the western side of the Muttama Creek whereas the Hume Highway today is on the eastern side. The creek itself runs behind the old Coolac Hotel, so one had to cross the creek behind the hotel to get to Gundagai.

The creek at the five mile site, known firstly as Splitters Creek and then as Sugar O'Briens Creek, is only small, and seldom flooded. When it did, it stayed up for only a day at a time. According to locals, not only could it have been navigated if one were desperate, but one seldom got bogged there.

By contrast, the Muttama Creek had a much larger catchment and stayed up for a week at a time.

The old Coolac Hotel is now the residence of the Cotterills, descendants of Coolac and Gundagai pioneers on both sides.

Cyril Sullivan's father was sure it all happened at the nine mile. Dianne and Kevin Cotteril live in the old Coolac Hotel, built in 1854. Dianne says they have had travellers call upon them who knew the hotel in the past, who told her the poem was written at that site.

One visitor she particularly remembers, in the early 1970s, was a Mrs Hargreaves who was on her way to Tumut. Mrs Hargreaves, a housemaid at the hotel at the turn of the century, claimed it was definitely there that the doggerel was written.

And well before the Dog monument was launched in 1932, a dog sitting on a tuckerbox was hoisted onto a rough pole attached to a fence post. This was proudly displayed in 1926 at the milestone marking the nine mile.

There are a small number of men and women who remember passing it, though none can remember who was responsible for it. At one stage it fell down, and was reinstated rather less grandly, at a lower level. It is the greatest of good fortune that Narelle Gillholme of Gundagai came across the photograph of it in an old family album (see frontispiece).

The local newspaper, the *Gundagai Independent*, wrote in its editorial of 11 August 1932, when discussion was still young in relation to the celebrations of the Back to Gundagai Week and the building of a monument to the pioneers:

> The emblem of our big week—monument to where the dog sat—There is not a person in the whole of Australia who has not heard of 'the dog and the tucker box' which is associated with the famous nine mile peg...

In the 1932 programme and souvenir booklet for Back to Gundagai Week, a number of the area's oldest pioneers are interviewed. One was John Keefe, born in 1844, who became a bullock driver at an early age. Mr Keefe stated:

> The favourite camping ground was a spot two or three miles past the well-known place, The Five Mile. It was impossible to camp anywhere near the present township site, as the thistles were that numerous and high there was a possibility of bullocks being lost for weeks.

(This would be relevant to spring and summer.)

So. With all this apparent evidence to confirm that the event happened, and the doggerel was written, nine miles from Gundagai, how is it that the locals insist that the episode of the Dog happened at the five mile site?

Before we go into the events surrounding that, we need an explanation of why the small town of Gundagai, with its crude doggerel about a dog, should have become famous.

The only way to gain fame is by spreading the word. There are three ways to spread the word. One is by voice, the other is the written word, and the last, and most important is in song.

Let's look into the three men who brought Gundagai fame by those means, *before* the Dog monument was launched in 1932.

4 Three Men who Brought Gundagai Fame

> The art of poetry is to touch the passions...
>
> Cowper

The poet and self-styled 'last of the bush troubadours', Jack Moses, is believed to be the originator of the name 'Bush Week' which refers to the week the country towns held their shows. He published two books of poems—*Beyond the City Gates*, and *Nine Miles from Gundagai*. (During the war he gave the proceeds of these books to the Red Cross for the war effort.)

Beyond the City Gates was published in 1923 and contained 'Nine Miles From Gundagai' which had been written in the 1880s. It was so well known that most people believed it was, and today still consider it to be, the first poem written on the subject. Many Gundagai residents even in 1932 were unsure who wrote the original poem.

Moses was born in 1860 and died in Sydney in July 1945. In an article written by him in 1938, he states he wrote 'Nine Miles from Gundagai' 50 years previously.

Sydney-born, Moses was a wine salesman, and his job took him into the country where he sold his wines (Caldwells) at the local shows, fairs and exhibitions. He travelled widely, and had a true liking for the bush and its people.

His obituary in a Sydney paper records:

...Jack had a chunky body, topped by a beaming dial whose eyes crinkled with good fellowship, he had a little table just inside or outside the pavilion. While your nose sported with the different mixture of smells coming from the cheese, bacon, honey, butter, preserves and so forth, he'd say, 'try this, boy—just a bit of God's sunshine from the land of milk and honey'. And you'd be holding a glass of good Australian wine.

At night, when the Show Society held its 'smoke social', the little man would be there, beaming like his own Australian sun, and reciting Nine Miles from Gundagai, or telling his yarn of how to improve bacon by crossing Berkshire sows with artesian bores. I suppose Jack Moses told that yarn on an average of once a week for 50 years, but it always brought the house down because its author was so sublimely confident that it would do so.

Nobody seems to remember when Jack Moses started 'doing' the Shows...but as he drifted through the country, and new generations grew to recognise him, he became an accepted feature of the rural scene.

When the whole blessed country was reciting his Nine Miles from Gundagai, and its 101 parodies, they'd meet the little man, and wait expectantly as though he were about to reel off some more catchy verses. And when it was quiet in the pavilion, he'd go and stand before the products of his country's earth and be moved to silent emotion.

I caught him twice in such moments. When I put a hand on his shoulder and asked 'How's she goin' Jack?', he turned; and there were the smile and the tears in his eyes and out came the words 'Boy, what a country!'. It was his theme song for over 50 years.

Advancing age and war restrictions stopped his travels, he took to hanging about the Arcadia in Pitt Street, or between the Metropole and the Royal Exchange, because he knew that country people favoured those spots and he was likely to meet men and women from the Monaro hills or the plains about Jerilderie...

He got more sheer happiness out of being Australian and seeing Australia and living Australia than any other man ever got out of achievement or money or love or victory in war.

Jack Moses—A rare character who loved Australia and the bush. His poem 'Nine Miles from Gundagai' and his variety of postcards perpetuated the myth of the Dog.

Jack Moses is dead at 85, his dream of Australia as 'the tuckerbox of the nations' unrealised but possible of fulfilment before he is forgotten. In him the bush has lost a friend and the nation a minor prophet.

Dan Clarke of Narrandera recalls Moses offering local resident, Locky Tindale, a drink. Tindale said he was teetotal. Moses replied, 'What a pity. You'll never know what it's like to be sober!'

Gundagai honoured Moses by naming a street after him: Moses Avenue. Although there was talk of erecting a statue in his honour at the nine mile peg, nothing came of the project.

A chapter on Jack Moses can't be written without repeating word-for-word what must be the greatest beat-up of all time. It was printed in the *Daily Advertiser* of Wagga Wagga on 10 October 1938.

Wagga's celebrations of Australia's sesquicentenary were imminent, and it is possible that Moses penned the article just to perpetuate the story of the Dog. Although Henry Lawson is given a by-line, he had been dead for 16 years.

There are two headings, the top one 'Nine Miles from Gundagai', with a subheading 'Bullock Driver's Romance'. Considering the high regard Moses had for country folk, he surely can't have believed they would swallow the storyline. Or was he just hoodwinking a gullible reporter?

By Henry Lawson and Jack Moses:

Strolling along the moonlit banks of the Murrumbidgee River near Gundagai, 40 years ago, two visitors to the show carnival of that town came upon a bullock-driver's outfit on the trek back from the railhead at Cootamundra. There they were entertained with singing and whip-cracking by the bullockies, and there these two famous men of Australian verse— Henry Lawson and Jack Moses—heard for the first time a detailed account by an Aborigine of the story of Gundagai's dog on the tucker-box.

Ten years previously Jack Moses had penned the nationwide known poem centring around a wisp of a story about the dog sitting on the box, which had without authentication become a by-word in the district of Gundagai.

The black boy's story was that years before he had come across a bullock driver's team standing near the river nine miles from Gundagai, and his dog sitting on the tucker-box.

The driver was missing. So the black ran to the Gundagai trooper to gain assistance to move the outfit from a rising flood.

When a party arrived at the scene everything had been swept away by the flooding river. 'Byemby a long time my countrymen find just bones of dog much down along river sitting up on tucker-box. Many feller my countrymen takem dog on box up and carry away along nine miles Gundagai that night. Big feller corroboree round dog on tucker-box. Never findem boss no time. Sweetheart makem very sad. She run away another white feller. White feller bullock team boss jump along river.'

It was a coincidence that Jack Moses should meet the black who vowed he had played such a prominent part in the drama, and that Moses in his poem should have written 'I've been jilted, jarred, and crossed in love, And sand-bagged in the dark'.

The contemporary story as concerned the whites at the time surrounding the dog on the tucker-box was more or less a phrase out of the dark and applying to any driver's dog on the Gundagai route, but the Aborigine's version is saturated with drama and romance. Generally the story could quite be accepted as truth, but even if it were not the old bullocky's dog has already found the limelight.

During that visit to Gundagai Henry Lawson was made a presentation of a smoker's outfit by the townspeople. He never forgot the generous-hearted 'Bidgee people, and in after years, on Jack Moses' return to Sydney from his annual visit, Lawson always asked how 'the boys' down south were getting along.

Jack Moses was one of Henry Lawson's closest friends,

and in that circle was called Jacky. In his tribute to Lawson after his death, in the book *Henry Lawson By His Mates*, Moses relates their visit to Gundagai, probably in the dying days of the 1800s or the early 1900s.

He tells how, during a stroll along the banks of the Murrumbidgee, the pair came across a drover's camp with a big mob of sheep. They sat and smoked with the drovers, and listened to their singing. One stood up and sang 'The Ballad of the Drover', but Lawson would not let Moses tell them who he was.

This experience appears to be the basis of the contrived story. Moses may have thought that involving an Aborigine in an explanation of the dog and tuckerbox story would give it some authenticity.

The theory that Moses wrote the above wildly outrageous account of the story of the origins of the Dog simply to perpetuate it is borne out by his statements in the *Daily Telegraph* article of 1938 which questioned who wrote 'Nine Miles from Gundagai'.

> They'll argue about whether I wrote it till Kingdom come…I wrote the poem all right. Somebody else might have done something like it before. I have never heard of it. *But I like them to argue about it. It keeps the poem alive.* They argue about whether it was five miles or nine miles, too. The 'nine-milers' would like to cut the throats of the 'five-milers' and so on.
>
> Up at Gundagai they asked me to change the words to five miles, because there's a pub there. They reckoned that Banjo Patterson, Lawson, and a couple of others wrote it. They've argued for 50 years about it. I reckon if they keep at it for another 50 years, the poem'll live for ever.

Well, it's more than 50 years…Who wrote the original doggerel may not be known, but it is clear that Moses wrote the second version which became famous. So there's not much argument there. There is though in the nine mile/five mile debate.

Moses was asked to change his poem to five miles

One of Jack Moses' postcards, on the back of which was printed the poem 'Nine Miles from Gundagai'.

from nine miles in a letter to him from the Gundagai Hospital Secretary in 1933.

After asking Moses if he would add one and a half pence to the cost of his card, which amount could be given to the hospital as a royalty, the writer, P.R. Kelly, goes on to say:

> The original poem, dated 1859, of which a printed copy is in the hands of a resident of Gundagai, shows the spot as '5 mile' not '9 mile', and in the old 'Times' Office, the original pull of your own shows also '5 Mile', so if possible I think it would be better if you could see your way to sanction that cards sold in Gundagai District show '5 Mile' instead of '9 Mile'.
>
> Sugar O'Brien's Creek is at the 5 mile, also the remains of the old 'Pub', which bears out that the 5 mile is the correct spot.

This request is remarkable in that this same man, Kelly, who was the organiser of the Back to Gundagai Week in 1932, was quite sure the correct location was at the nine mile before the decision was made to erect the monument at the five mile.

And it is just one example of how he and others moved to squash the possibility that the doggerel was written about the nine mile crossing, in order to justify locating the monument at the five mile site.

Moses' reply came through his partner, Austral Press & Advertising Ltd, Sydney, who shared the copyright with him.

> ...Now with regard to the alteration of the wording from 'Nine' to 'Five' Mr Moses does not wish to do this as, for as far back as 50 years, he has been distributing and reciting the poem throughout the Commonwealth in the way it appears now. Also in the original drama written by Arthur Steery the word 'nine' appeared.

There are two points in this response which are of interest. If Moses had written the poem 'as far back as 50 years', that takes it to 1883. Other reports date it at 1888 at the earliest. And just who Arthur Steery was, is perplexing. Could he have been the actual writer of the doggerel, or did he write a play on the subject. If so, what happened to it?

And concerning the paragraph in the letter by Kelly to Moses, referring to 'the original pull of your own shows also 5 Mile', here we have the first hint that type was changed at the newspaper to authenticate the five mile site.

This is the only document I have seen that says that Moses' poem was printed in the *Gundagai Times*, although that would have been quite normal. But there's no way he would have written 'five miles', because it was not an issue in the 1880s, nor even in the 1890s, assuming it was not immediately published.

The introduction of the five mile site came up only during 1932.

Herald, Hargus, Hage!

Such was the cry of Gundagai's supersalesman, Ephraim Close O'Sullivan, newsagent extraordinaire, as he strode the platform of the railway station at Gundagai.

Born in 1879, he had seven children by his wife Ester Harpley. When she died in 1935, he brought up the children on his own.

He showed real initiative in that he reproduced Jack Moses' poem onto a 'piece of cardboard with a drawing of a dog on the other side' and sold it to passengers on the numerous trains which went through Gundagai.

O'Sullivan's daughter, Muriel Whitmore, recalls:

In those days, nearly every commercial traveller travelled by train. My father met every train to sell newspapers and the poem. Slowly but surely the poem's fame spread.

To my father is given the credit for the circulation of Moses' poem and its subsequent adoption by Australians.

However, my father omitted to get Moses' permission to do this, and Jack took him to court for infringement of copyright. The court case had no effect on their friendship which lasted until Moses' death.

Ephraim O'Sullivan's newsagency is in the background extreme left in this turn of the century shot taken by famous Gundagai photographer Dr Gabriel of residents assembling for a parade. (Courtesy Cliff Butcher, Gundagai historian)

One of the original Moses postcards depicting a bullock team, the Dog, and nine miles. (Courtesy National Library, Canberra)

In June 1925 O'Sullivan agreed to pay Moses £22. 2*s*.6*d*. in four equal monthly instalments which he finalised in October of that year, receiving a deed of release for his pains.

As well as his habit of adding an 'h' rather than dropping it as was customary, another cry O'Sullivan used at the station to sell his papers and magazines was '*Man* two shillings, *Woman* three pence. Happy married couple, two shillings and three pence'.

In the booklet, *The Tender Years*, Jack Bell writes:

E.C. O'Sullivan had a bookstall at the railway station. To see him selling newspapers was a real revelation. Up and down the platform, in low key and high, he revelled in reciting Nine Miles from Gundagai. 'Gundy' used lots of punchlines and some funny capers, believing, of course, it could be fun selling papers.

Any person who used trains between 1917 and 1960, up to two weeks before his death, would remember him.

In the book *Australian Folklore* compiled by Bill

Ephraim C. O'Sullivan, newsagent and first real promoter of the Dog legend through postcards sold at the Gundagai and Narrandera railway stations.

Wannan and published by Lansdowne Press in 1970,
there is a phrase 'No good to Gundy', meaning something
that has no value, is absolutely worthless. Although
Gundagai has been referred to as Gundy in print, Wannan
failed to find the origin of the expression, wondering if
it was a small country town. It's not beyond the realm
of possibility that it related to O'Sullivan. Considering
his reputation as a salesman, anything that had no
value, and couldn't be sold, would be 'no good to Gundy!'

> Names memorable long,
> If there be force in virtue or in song.
>
> Pope

Jack O'Hagan was born in Melbourne in 1898, 10–15 years
after Jack Moses wrote the poem of the Dog. And he
published the song 'Along the Road to Gundagai' the year
Henry Lawson died—1922. Second only to 'Waltzing Matilda'
as Australia's most popular song, one hundred thousand
copies of the sheet music were sold in the first two years.

Among the 600 songs O'Hagan wrote, 200 have been
published or recorded.

In 1937 he wrote the song 'Where the Dog sits on the
Tuckerbox'. Also known as 'My Mabel Waits for Me', it
refers to Dave's girlfriend in Australia's second longest
running, and highly popular radio serial, 'Dad and Dave',
which was already using 'Along the Road to Gundagai'
as its theme song. A spin-off of this was that Snake
Gully, the home of Dad and Dave in Steele Rudd's book,
now became accepted as being in Gundagai at the
Tuckerbox site.

In 1942, O'Hagan wrote 'When a Boy from Alabama
meets a Girl from Gundagai', a delightful tune which
O'Hagan told Gundagai historian Cliff Butcher 'was his
favourite song'.

'Along the Road to Gundagai' has won the district
publicity unequalled by any other country centre in
Australia—indeed any city or region of Australia. It has
been sung in music halls in New York, London and Paris,
and was whistled by the diggers.

Jack O'Hagan at work in the 1950s.

The famous Australian singer Peter Dawson was the first person to make a recording of it. This was done in London, as Australia had no recording facilities then.

There can be no better way to keep a city or town in the public's mind, and create a mystique about it, than by perpetuating it in song. Gundagai knows how fortunate it is that Jack O'Hagan nominated the town in his song.

Bundaberg was O'Hagan's first choice for a location. But he was looking for a river with a romantic sound to it, and the local Burnett River didn't suit. He turned instead to the Murrumbidgee as more appealing, and substituted Gundagai for Bundaberg.

It was 1956 before Jack O'Hagan set foot in Gundagai, the year of the Olympic Games in Melbourne. Oscar Hammerstein II was visiting Australia. (His wife Dorothy Blanchard was Australian.) He and O'Hagan had become good friends. Hammerstein was to tell O'Hagan that he himself hadn't seen the Mississippi River when he wrote 'Old Man River', and neither had Stephen Foster seen the Swanee River. So he was in good company—making a region famous through song without having seen it.

O'Hagan was the honoured guest of Gundagai for a week when the new tourist centre at the Tuckerbox site was opened by then Premier Cahill. He also has a street in Gundagai named after him.

Jack O'Hagan was an acclaimed songwriter, composing songs for movies. His first big hit was in 1920—the prelude for a silent movie, *The Affairs of Anatol*, starring Gloria Swanson. His next was 'In Dreamy Araby', for the Rudolph Valentino film, *The Sheik*.

He narrowly missed having his song 'God Bless Australia' chosen as our national anthem. It was written to the tune of 'Waltzing Matilda'. Woolworths sold over 30 000 records through their stores, and Ampol sold another half million through their service stations.

One song, 'Mexican Serenade', was the first ever recorded in English by the great Richard Tauber. And who doesn't know 'Our Don Bradman'.

Jack O'Hagan died in 1987, and although the Melbourne Performing Arts Museum paid him a tribute in 1984, I have yet to see a book in the library celebrating his works or his life.

Right to left: Jack O'Hagan, C.B. Stribley, president, Gundagai Shire Council, Mrs Josephine O'Hagan and Major C.W. Bayliss, president, Services Club, during O'Hagan's 1956 visit to Gundagai—his first.

5 A Plan for a Monument

News is conveyed by letter, word or mouth,
And comes from North, East, West and South.

The newsagent Ephraim O'Sullivan was the first person (other than Moses himself) to actively publicise Moses' poem of the Dog through the sale of the cards he produced.

O'Sullivan decided to go for greater stakes, and run a newsagency in Wagga Wagga. So he sold his shop in 1931, taking his stock of postcards with him. (He sold them in Wagga Wagga, and also in Narrandera, where he established himself for the rest of his life.)

Oscar Collins owned the other newsagency. He soon found that travellers to Gundagai wanted to know where the Dog was situated. A natural promoter, and fortified by his overseas experiences (already discussed), he was frustrated by his inability to satisfy them.

Charles Cork owned the Ford service station (later Gundagai Motors) in 1931. Collins would have a yarn with Cork daily as he walked past his garage. 'People are always asking me where's the tuckerbox. We should get a box and make one, and make postcards from that, and raise money for the hospital,' he'd say.

Cork says he remembers the site was out at the nine mile. 'There was only a notice there, this side of the Coolac Hotel. It was rough, and had been hoisted on the fence, by a local. Oscar said to me "it's too far out", so they brought it in to the present site.' [This last was of course after all the negotiations had been finalised in late 1932]. Cork continued, 'There was no real controversy at the time. It was all agreed in the end.'

That may sound a simplification of the issue, but although there was debate, it is remarkable how easily the town accepted that the 5 mile site was the most suitable, and therefore the 'right' one.

On 29 July 1932 the first *public* meeting was held to discuss the Back to Gundagai week and the erection of a monument to the pioneers in the form of a dog on a tuckerbox.

The first move was to carry the resolution that the 'Week' was being held with the object of clearing debt from the Gundagai District Hospital. It was plainly understood that the affair would be the biggest event ever held in Gundagai. Mr Percy R. Kelly was appointed organiser of the scheme.

The *Gundagai Independent*'s editorial of 11 August 1932 stated:

> There is not a person in the whole of Australia who has not heard of the Dog and the Tuckerbox, which is associated with the famous nine mile peg. Year upon year, thousands of cards are sold, on which are printed Jack Moses' poetry, and that author collects a royalty on each. But before Jack Moses wrote this poem, the dog and the tuckerbox were well known.
>
> A monument should be erected at the nine mile peg, dedicated to the pioneers and bullockys, who made the highway of today possible. And there should be an unveiling ceremony during the Back to Gundagai week.
>
> Here's where the hospital will benefit. When a solid concrete structure is erected, a photo of the monument could be taken and placed on cards for sale, with a 2d royalty to the institution. To say that the monument would not pay for itself, and ever afterwards not bring in cash for the hospital, is wrong.

From 2000 to 4000 of the present cards are sold annually, and a 2d royalty on 2000 cards would add over 16 pounds per annum to the finances of the hospital.

Let us make the pilgrimage to the tuckerbox and the unveiling of the monument, the big thing in connection with our Back to Gundagai week. It is up to us to see that one of the most historic spots in the Commonwealth, not only brings finance to our hospital, but is adorned with a monument that will forever be something to show that Gundagai has not forgotten its pioneers and bullockys, who made present day life possible.

Kelly wrote a letter to the paper on 22 August 1932:

Sir: Now that at long last it has been decided to erect a monument to perpetuate the memory of our pioneers, it would be of interest, if, through your columns the much discussed question of site could be settled. As the general opinion outside of Gundagai is that the historic event occurred at the present nine mile peg, I am personally very much in favour of erecting a monument there. However, a discussion through your valued paper would be of great interest. Yours etc.

Weeks later, on 12 September 1932, another editorial: 'SHIRE TURNS DEAF EAR TO PROPOSITION—Will not give grant for monument'.

Upon the refusal of the Gundagai Shire to associate itself with the most historic attraction of the 'Week', it has to a certain extent, poured 'cold water' on the biggest boost Gundagai could possibly have.

We are surprised that one of our town councillors absolutely wanted to squash the project, and that our other representative did not support the motion to erect the monument.

Gundagai, don't let this little punch knock you over. Come back stronger than ever. Erect the monument and put this district in the forefront of all New South Wales.

The report goes on to say that Messrs Stribley and Collins, representing the Week committee, had approached the council and asked for financial assistance. They explained that the aim of their delegation 'is that a monument be placed at the 5 mile peg'. There had been considerable interest by the Sydney press for information and photos. The cost for the erection of the monument they said would be about £65. There was to be a competition for the best verse applicable to the occasion, which would be attached to the monument.

Council discussed the matter when Collins and Stribley retired. The first remark by a councillor was 'we have no money for roads, therefore we have no money for monuments'. Three councillors then said they were in support of the motion to grant funds. But the next three speakers were quite sure they wanted nothing to do with it. On the division, only three voted with the motion: Crs Hyndes, McHugh and Luff.

Without further public discussion, it appears that the committee decided to raise funds themselves, and erect the monument at the five mile peg. The 26 September edition of the paper reported:

> A well attended meeting of the Central committee was held on Thursday last. It was definitely decided to immediately go ahead with the monument, and that *permission be obtained to erect* same at the five mile peg opposite the old hotel.

The paper goes on to state that 'several letters from very old identities of Gundagai were read, and provided very interesting reading'. These letters were not reproduced in the paper, although this was a common habit of the time. Perhaps they all supported the nine mile site?

By this time, Gundagai was getting a lot of kudos in the city papers for being the first town in Australia to make the move to honour our pioneers.

It isn't hard to imagine Oscar Collins' mind at work now. With all the best intentions under the sun, for the good of Gundagai and its hospital, he felt he had to bury the nine milers for good.

He had to go to the original source, the only final, indisputable, evidence that the original doggerel said 'nine miles'. He had to go to the local newspaper offices, find the blocks used, and alter them.

The unsubstantiated story goes that Collins and a compositor at the *Times* altered each 'n' to an 'f' and a 'v'. They allegedly worked all night because steel blocks were used in those days for type. If this story is true, it means that the issue which had the doggerel in was in Gundagai in 1932. As that issue is not at the libraries, it also means that whoever came up with the date 20 June 1859 could have fabricated that date to cloud the issue.

If it were in fact Collins, it was not done from any personal motive. From the hospital's point of view the closer location was far, far better than the nine mile site.

One can also understand that in those days the distance of five miles away from Gundagai was formidable, as not many had cars, so nine miles would have seemed twice as formidable.

In the weeks prior to the launching, the local paper requested 'everybody who has a car, lorry, cart, sulky, buggy or any other conveyance, please be in town on Monday 28th, at 9 am and help to convey children to 5 mile, for unveiling of Pioneer's Monument'.

6 Rusconi's Commission

I have been pursued, dogged and waylaid.

Pope

There was no need to look elsewhere than to Frank Rusconi to oversee the erection of the Dog monument.

That brilliant artisan had been living in Gundagai since 1906. His dream was to promote Australian marble as being among the world's best, which it was then and still is today.

After training in the marble trade in both Switzerland and Italy, Rusconi returned to Australia in 1901. In 1910 he collected as many pieces as he possibly could of different Australian marbles, to build a marble mansion in miniature, as a showcase for Australian marble.

His masterpiece, which took 28 years to complete, is on show in Gundagai. Rusconi has always been credited with 'modelling' the Dog, but even this does not appear to be accurate.

Rusconi sent to Sydney to have the foundry work done, as the Dog was to be cast in bronze. Rusconi's son Peter recalls that they cast a model and sent it back to him for his approval.

The name of the foundry was Olivers in Alexandria. Five years before, in 1927, Olivers had been bought by W.J. Treloar and it wasn't until the mid-50s that the company's name was changed to Treloar Manufacturing Pty Ltd.

Rusconi's masterpiece in marble took 28 years to complete. No plans or drawings of any kind were used, and 20 varieties of marble went into the work of art.

The dog was cast in bronze—a mixture of 83% copper, 5% each tin, zinc and lead, and 2% copper phosphate. Alfred Taylor of Punchbowl, the man on staff who cast the Dog, won renown for his work. He was a master craftsman who had already earned recognition throughout the industry for his skill at casting.

In a letter written by Rosalie Odell, granddaughter of Frederick McGowan, to the Gundagai Shire Council in 1985, she says:

> My grandfather Frederick McGowan died in 1941, but my grandmother always told me that he sculpted the actual figure of the Dog on the Tuckerbox. She used to tell me about my mother being sent next door to borrow their dog to pose and details such as my mother getting roused on because she couldn't make the dog sit still.

Yet Percy Kelly is quoted in the *Sunday Telegraph* of

September 1963 as saying that he organised to have the 'bronze dog cast from a photograph'.

An article in the *Sunday Telegraph* of 25 August 1963 headed 'THAT TUCKERBOX DOG—Its creator is sick of it' confirms that Rusconi did not design the dog model, although he certainly did the foundation.

Frank Rusconi, who built the Dog on the Tuckerbox five miles from Gundagai, vowed on his 89th birthday this week he would never go near the world-famous monument again.

He said the monument was in the wrong place, and the bullock teamsters who inspired the story would never have a dog like the one that now sits on the Tuckerbox.

Mr Rusconi was commissioned by the organising committee to build the Dog monument.

The dog was cast in Sydney to the drawings of a dog the organisers provided.

'I don't know what sort of dog it is supposed to be,' he said. 'All I know is that no bullock team would have a dog looking like that.'

Mr Rusconi goes on to say, rather bitterly, that he wanted the dog placed in front of the ruins of the hotel at the site, and that it was he who had suggested a monument to the Dog, four years before the organising committee adopted the idea.

He had not been to see the monument for years, 'and I've no desire to ever go near it again.'

That Rusconi first suggested a monument of the Dog is borne out in a taped radio interview when he said that he had suggested the idea to the hospital board four years before they took up the idea.

It is not surprising that Mr Rusconi was rather disappointed with the whole affair.

However, the foundry, Olivers-cum-W.J. Treloar & Sons, were very happy with their involvement, naming the statue of the Dog as their 'most famous product'. In July 1987 they celebrated the company's 60 years in business by producing a limited number of replicas of the original miniature, which were presented to guests at their anniversary celebrations.

Strangely, the original photograph of the Dog Treloar's have in their offices shows the dog on the tuckerbox sitting on a second block of concrete inscribed 'Pioneers Monument Gundagai'. Yet photographs of it in place in Gundagai show that this block was left out when the monument was launched in 1932. It does reappear later, and is part of the monument today. (See photographs below and on p.14.)

1937—Judith Evans of Leeton found this in the family album—the ladies identified are Mrs Mapletoft and Mrs Wairs. Note that the foundation does not have 'Pioneer Monument Gundagai' engraved on it, although the original photograph in Treloar's offices does, and the monument standing today does include it.

7 The Monument Unveiled

He soon equips the ships, supplies the sails,
And gives the word to launch.

Dryden

The unveiling ceremony on 28 November 1932 also marked the 103rd anniversary of the founding of Gundagai by Captain Sturt. The prime minister, Joe Lyons, had agreed to do the unveiling—his first visit to Gundagai, indeed the first by a prime minister.

By this time the Gundagai Shire, which had wanted no part of the Dog in the first place, was quick to state that they would give a civic reception and luncheon for the prime minister, in honour of his visit.

The town of Gundagai for the preceding week was awash with Back To festivities of every nature; sporting, racing, balls, street fairs, band recitals, picnics and processions.

When Miss Grace Luff was crowned queen, the money she and the other candidates had raised was more than enough to clear the hospital of debt.

A nation-wide competition for an inscription of 30 words in verse epitomising the pluck and hardships of the pioneers had been won. Brian Fitzpatrick of Sydney, chief leader-writer of the *World*, won seven guineas for his effort. The Back To committee offered two guineas, and Sydney's *Daily Telegraph* added five more.

The inscription on the monument reads:

Earth's self upholds this monument
    To conquerors who won her when
Wooing was dangerous, and now
    Are gathered unto her again.

This was not an event to be missed. All the relevant politicians, mayors and shire presidents were attending in their official capacities. Cinesound Productions was sending a cameraman to take 'talkie pictures'. All Sydney newspapers were sending reporters, and '57 broadcasting stations, both A and B are putting on a special session', as well as talking about Gundagai all week, and naturally playing 'Along the Road to Gundagai'.

It was, as the newspaper articles said, 'a week that will go down in history as one where Gundagai set the lead for the rest of Australia to follow, in remembering what our Pioneers did for us'.

The press was even suggesting that there should be a national holiday—Pioneers Day. And pioneering women were not forgotten.

The *Gundagai Independent* of 20 October 1932, in its editorial, said:

> Let it never be out of mind that you cannot discuss Australian pioneering and leave the women out. There was Caroline Chisholm, who on horseback, took the migrant domestics from Sydney out on to the stations; Caroline Chisholm, who for her services to immigration and this young colony, was honoured by the British Government; Caroline Chisholm always went unmolested by the bushrangers—her goodness and greatness were recognised even by them. And there were those countless other women who carried on when sickness or death struck their menfolk down, and who, through the long, danger-filled years, proved themselves splendid Mates of Men.

At last the special moment was upon them.

A hot sun beamed from a cloudless sky, and overhead

two aeroplanes flew, as along the bitumen surfaced highway there passed the procession from historic Gundagai to the famous Five Mile peg. Bells pealed, the crowd cheered, the bands played, motor sirens tooted, horses pranced, and all was a scene of emotion.

As that mass of humanity flowed down Sheridan Street, it resembled an army going forth... At the end of Sheridan Street, a brief halt was taken, whilst bandsmen, firemen, scouts, school children and others scrambled into waiting motor lorries and cars, and again the pilgrims moved on...

'Advance Australia Fair' was played as the bands

The unveiling of the Dog on the Tuckerbox monument by the then prime minister Joe Lyons on 28 November 1932. Handing over the bottle is Tom Collins, member for Hume. Bill Stribley, hospital board chairman, is in the foreground at right, while E.C. O'Sullivan is to the immediate right of Collins.

approached the monument, where nearby was a bullock team, yoked to a waggon loaded with wood.

> As the Prime Minister, Mr Lyons, approached, the band struck up Australia's own song, and the crowd of nearly three thousand people burst forth in cheers.

A handful of local pioneers were given positions of prominence, including 'Granny' Luff, 90, the oldest white woman in the community, who had come to Gundagai in 1870; and George Fox, 87, who joined Cobb & Co. as a coach driver in 1877.

Mr Lyons thanked Gundagai for the honour of unveiling the monument, and said he was glad that 'a few of that splendid band of early settlers had been spared, and were able to reap some of the benefits of modern civilisation'.

Speaking later at the civic luncheon, Mr Lyons said:

> If party bitterness was killed and everyone was willing to strive towards a common goal, many of the difficulties with which the Commonwealth was faced, could be overcome...Today people do not show sufficient self-reliance, and seek too readily the aid of Governments. When the people become ever more ready to lean on Governments, they were coming very close to Communism. Let us follow the example of the pioneers, who fought their own difficulties, and won through.

8 Anne of Snake Gully

Every moment alters what is done,
And innovates some act till then unknown.

Dryden

Enter Anne of Snake Gully.

Ada Heath was sitting under a gum tree with her mother, watching the unveiling of the Dog monument in 1932, when Anne, then aged 48, eyed the area, and declared she was assessing where her house was to be built.

'I'm going to set up a souvenir shop and tea rooms,' Anne declared. 'And I will look after the monument.' She was as good as her word.

Anne Elizabeth Skinner was born at Wagga Wagga in 1884. As a young girl she moved to Sydney where she sold spectacles. There she met her first husband, Ben Ridding, and married him in 1903 at the age of 19.

She had six children, and suffered ill health when they were very young. They lived in Redfern, and there Annie, as she was called, opened her first shop. Ben had become ill and could do only light work.

When the First World War started, Annie made the decision to move next to the Liverpool army camp. There she opened a shop and made money from the soldiers, sending her young sons into the camp to sell cigarettes, drinks and lollies.

Later she opened a laundry and went into the camp collecting the soldiers' washing. Her children helped, or didn't eat.

She also provided entertainment for the soldiers, employing 'an old doctor who had drunk himself out of his profession' to play piano while soldiers and officers sang and danced the nights away. In 1921 Ben Ridding died.

As the army base had slowly emptied, Annie decided to sell her shops and leave for the bush, where, she had heard, more work was to be found for her boys. In an old BSA truck with canopy, and six children, Annie set off to make their fortunes. At each town they sought work, but the answer was always no.

Food, money and petrol were nearly depleted when they arrived in Young in time for cherry picking. They all worked hard and made a lot of money. They felt like millionaires after being so broke.

She then opened a boarding house for the workers constructing a weir nearby. For six years they lived there, until the weir was completed. Then they moved on to where a bridge was being constructed. She opened up a shop there, as well as a tuckshop at the nearby Yanco agricultural college.

When this was finished, they again upped stakes— this time to the sound of 'gold' at Gundagai. Gold was not plentiful, so Annie opened a dress shop. She also took on the mail run, and was the first person to drive children to school—in a truck.

At Liverpool, Anne had met Andy Pyers who wanted to marry her. She said no because she didn't want her children to have a stepfather. But if he would wait until her youngest, George, was 21, she would marry him then. In 1933, Annie sent Andy a telegram saying she would marry him now. He came down to Gundagai where they were married.

Annie had already negotiated for land and the right to open the souvenir shop. They built a house at the monument site, and also opened tea rooms. The amenities were crude. The souvenir stand was a small corrugated iron shed, closed on three sides and open towards the highway.

Annie also sold her souvenirs from a tray which she

carried, supported by a strap around her neck. Those souvenirs consisted of matchbox covers with a picture and verse, postcards, and a folder of Gundagai views.

Outside the tea rooms, Andy Pyers put a box which he labelled 'tuckerbox'. They taught their dog Hoppy to sit on it, and pose for the benefit of tourists and photographers, rewarding him with a biscuit.

In 1937 the 'Dad and Dave' radio serial, set in 'Snake Gully' began. The theme song chosen for the national serial was 'Along the Road to Gundagai'.

The couple named their shop and tea rooms Snake Gully, and started telling visitors that they were 'Dad' and 'Mum'. They would point to nearby farmhouses, saying that that was where the serial's other characters lived—Bill Smith here and Dave and Mabel there, and so on. It is said they got so good at it that they started to believe it themselves. (The Steele Rudd characters have been reproduced in copper at the tuckerbox site.)

Annie Pyers with dog Hoppy outside her tea rooms in the 1940s. Hoppy would sit on a box with the word 'tuckerbox' painted on it and pose for photographers.

Dad, Dave, Mum and Mabel of Snake Gully are now part of the Tuckerbox tourist centre.

It was Annie who put in the wishing well in front of the Dog, for the benefit of the Gundagai Hospital. She would carry suitcases full of money into the secretary of the hospital, and she always put a thankyou notice next to the Dog so that tourists would know how much had been raised.

Anne Pyers was a natural wheeler-dealer. She sold a hat off her own head, and once bought a truck which had broken down in front of her home. She sold it two days later for twice the price.

Charles Cork recalls,

One day Annie Pyers came in with a biscuit tin and bought a new Ford touring car. In that tin she had ten shilling notes—probably 500 of them! Another time, she came over to my father, who was very strict, never smoked or drank, and said, 'Mr Cork, I have a riddle I made up. What has four letters, starts with F and makes your back sore?' Father blushed and she laughingly said, 'A Ford!'

Gundagai had no ambulance in those days, so Annie would often drive her Ford V8 to Sydney with patients. Once when speeding at Goulburn she was pulled up by police. When she gave her address as Snake Gully, the police thought she was being smart, and insisted on proof. They finally let her off with a warning.

At the time of petrol rationing during World War II, Annie seemed to be able to cope. When asked how she managed for fuel, she replied: 'Some people use V for victory. I used P for petrol.'

Anne Pyers' life changed when Andy suddenly died. She tried to stay at the shop and tea rooms, but it was too lonely. She sold out to George and Dorrie Smith in 1950.

Annie eventually went back to Liverpool, and died there at the age of 72.

9 Trek to the Tuckerbox

And pile up every stone
Of lustre from the brook in memory
Or monument to ages.

Milton

By July 1933 it was perceived there was a need to
enclose the monument with a fence. Cyclone Fence &
Gate Co., Sydney, quoted £11. 14s. plus sales tax of 14 s.
1d. (6 per cent). The fence was to be of chain wire mesh
with galvanised pipe set in concrete, of which the top
12 inches would be drilled to carry two rows of barbed
wire.

Apart from the erection of two outhouses in 1947,
the monument was left as it was, until in 1948 the
Hospital Board, which was responsible for its upkeep,
realised that something had to be done to 'turn it into
a really beautiful site, befitting the publicity it has
received'.

They decided to immediately plant trees and replace
those that had died, build a kiosk with proper floorings
and conveniences, and paint and repair the fence around
the monument. This was not done.

When George Smith and his wife Dorrie bought the
business from Annie Pyers in 1950, Mrs Smith took up
the sale of souvenirs. She didn't drive, so George would
drive her to the souvenir shed and leave her there all
day while he went about his work. Their daughter Ann

circa *1950—Local families the Schofields and the Wearns pose in front of the monument. Hollyhocks grow inside the fence, planted by Annie Pyers in an attempt to beautify the site.*

1950—George Smith, who took over the souvenir stand from Annie Pyers, has obviously cleared out the flowers.

Ann Smith in 1954, posed with a soldier visitor to the memorial in front of the tin shed which was used as the Tuckerbox souvenir stand. Ann did her share of selling souvenirs, and remembers 'counting many thousands of coins, mainly pennies' which had been thrown into the wishing well at the monument, which stood on the Gundagai side of the shed.

1955—Mr McDonald (right) owner of champion racehorse Toporoa, stopped on the way home to capture on film one great Aussie emblem—the 1955 Melbourne Cup won by Toparoa—with another, and even older—the Dog.

Cabban recalls, 'the shed was hot and dusty in summer and cold in winter, but business was good and a great deal of souvenirs were sold. We counted many thousands of coins from the wishing well, mainly pennies.'

In wintertime their only heat was a kerosene heater. When it got dark, and too cold, Dorrie didn't wait for George to come back. She'd load the souvenirs in the old Chevy car he'd left there and push it down the road to their house, which at the time was where the train stop restaurant now is.

By early 1955 the authorities were concerned that travellers stopping to photograph the monument were 'dangerously close to fast traffic on the nearby highway', and the monument was moved back a short distance.

As an indication of the extent to which the myth of the Dog had caught the imagination of Australians, the turnout in 1956 for the opening of the newly erected kiosk and unveiling of a plaque numbered 8000 people.

This ceremony, conducted by then premier of New South Wales, J.J. Cahill, less than 24 years after the launch of the Dog monument, surpassed that momentous event.

It, too, was held in conjunction with a Back to Gundagai week.

The Hume Highway was closed for an hour and a half while the 'colossal crowd, huge procession and 2247 motor vehicles' travelled to the five mile site. The *Gundagai Independent* reported:

> Never in the imagination of the organisers was it expected that the trek to the Tuckerbox would reach such magnificent proportions. The parade was the entire length of Gundagai's main street...old model cars, buggies, spring carts, phaetons and sulkies, and then to add that touch of real Australian glamour came the hoof beats of horses—a noise reminiscent of the days of yore.
>
> And to bring back this past, one hundred and fifty horsemen and horsewomen rode four abreast in a most stirring and appealing display...
>
> On arrival at the Tuckerbox site, the floats lined

Prior to 1956, before the Dog was moved to stand in front of the newly built kiosk. This close-up shows the Pioneers' Wishing Well. Visitors are invited to 'Throw in a coin and wish'. All proceeds to the Gundagai Hospital.

The opening of the new kiosk by J.J. Cahill, premier of N.S.W. in April 1956. On the right are Bob Stribley, Gundagai Shire president, and Bill Sheahan, member for Burrinjuck.

up outside the park, and the bullock team was driven to the side of the road. The hundred and fifty horsemen formed a long single file alongside the bitumen, led by Arch Stuckey of Tarrabandra, a grandson of the first white settler to take up land on the southern side of the Murrumbidgee River at Gundagai.

The scene at the old teamsters' camping ground was amazing. It was a scene that will never be forgotten by any person who witnessed the stupendous spectacle. It was the greatest tribute to the early settlers ever paid by any community in the Commonwealth.

Premier Cahill declared,

I had no idea that I would witness such an amazing and inspiring spectacle as that which presents itself at this very moment. I am deeply moved at the magnificent manifestation of gratitude you now pay to the Pioneers.

It is fitting that we should all cooperate in public acknowledgement of the worth and the work of those hardy people who blazed the trail for those who have come after them. Your earliest settlers were men and women of unbounded courage and faith in the destiny of their country and of themselves. They won through and gained a heritage for themselves and for those who came after...

10 Shall We Move It?

Those who came after...did not always treat the Dog monument with respect.

The site became so dilapidated that residents were writing to the local paper protesting at the neglect of the pioneers' monument. One resident in 1960, said, 'I sometimes wonder whether the people of Gundagai realise that we have the best known and most historic spot in Australia at our front door. We do nothing to make it more interesting and attractive, and nothing to make it more impressive. We certainly do not show respect or honour our pioneers.'

In 1962, plans were made for a unique nature park at the site. Local businesses, the chamber of commerce, local shire council and Sydney City Council, which offered expertise in lieu of money, were involved.

During 1963 the plans were altered, but by September the first sod was turned in the plan to convert the six acres adjacent to the memorial into 'Australia's only native parkland, incorporating ferns to giant trees'. Australian animals were to be introduced later. There would be a maze, and a boomerang-shaped rockery. The ruins of the old inn would be preserved, and a giant glasshouse constructed to house the Australian native flowers display.

A press conference was held in Sydney 'to announce to the world what Gundagai intends doing with the park'. The sod-turning ceremony was televised by the ABC, and the *Bulletin* ran a story on it. There was a big roll-up of councillors and prominent businessmen.

It was expected to be completed by Christmas 1963, but the much vaunted project fell through, and the only improvement made was a large Australian fernhouse, set up in 1965 at a cost of $22 000.

Even so, when the highway bypass was mooted, the 'enhancements' to the monument site brought this protest from a letter-writer:

A recent trip to Melbourne by road after many years brought me one of those shattering moments of disillusionment which darken a day. I had always remembered that little monument to a piece of Australian folklore, sitting forlornly, but meaningfully, on a grassy road-side patch. Now it tries to dominate, ineptly, a tourist reserve where 'attractions' include an irrelevant fernhouse.

If the expressway is built, it will be a pity I know, but it serves everyone right for spoiling my 'image' of the dog.

The greatest uproar came when the Gundagai tourist promotion committee requested a 'referendum' to determine if residents wanted the Dog monument shifted from its site into the town of Gundagai.

On Saturday, 14 February 1976 the residents of the Shire of Gundagai were asked to answer one question: 'Do you approve of the removal of the Dog on the Tuckerbox statue from the present site at the Five Mile to a site in or near the town of Gundagai?'

The question of moving the Dog had been a controversial one for years. The imminent bypass of the town by the Hume Highway had prompted a decision to be made.

Those wanting the move were inspired by pure economic motives—ensuring that tourist traffic be attracted into Gundagai after the bypass. 'The future of Gundagai will be grim indeed. The choice the people make will determine whether Gundagai will grow or dwindle, and become another by-passed village of considerably lower population.'

Those opposed said it was given its place by legend

and history; one local going so far as to say it would be like 'shifting the tower of Pisa to Venice'.

The issue attracted national press. Radio and television arrived in Gundagai to interview and film locals. The local paper received letters from all states of Australia.

One, in stating that the Dog should be moved, said it would be fitting for it to be placed in an attractive historical setting.

> Its present position does nothing to enhance its significant historical interest. If the Dog is moved into town, then more of the story of early Australia will be noted. It is an insult to the intelligence of the Australian tourist to be offered lollies, drinks and other material goods as an alternative to information about his own past.

One correspondent from South Australia even suggested that the statue be moved—but to the nine mile site.

One opposing the move wondered if one would move a war memorial, while another referred to 'the ghouls who are attempting to debase the Monument to the pioneers'; they would make 'Gundagai gain only contempt by trying to use it to make a few dollars'.

On voting day, there was an overwhelming rejection of the suggestion that the monument should be moved. Only those in the immediate vicinity of Gundagai voted. The outlying polling booths were not opened. Altogether 991 people voted, representing 40 per cent of those eligible. Only 19.77 per cent were in favour of the move.

Tradition and the legend of the Dog won the day.

One newspaper's editorial, in applauding the people of Gundagai for rejecting the move, said 'in this speeding world of sometimes mindless change' it was reassuring to know that, 'though Fraser may come and Whitlam may go, the dog sits on the tuckerbox five miles from Gundagai'.

On Thursday morning, 22 October 1981, when Jerry Sheahan, the proprietor of the service station on the tuckerbox site, was serving his first customer, he was asked 'what happened to the Dog?'

Having had his own dog run down by a car the previous day, he said 'It was run over yesterday', completely unaware that THE DOG had gone missing. It was neither in, nor on, the tuckerbox. It had been 'alf-inched!

The usual culprits who pull stupid tricks of this type were to blame.

University students from the campus of the Canberra College of Advanced Education had taken the Dog as a 'Stone Day' prank. A phone call the following day to the ABC revealed that the Dog was safe.

The interest which the prank had created was enormous. National press, radio and TV inundated Gundagai for interviews and news. The police at Belconnen who recovered the Dog set it up outside their station. When Gundagai residents came to pick it up, 'the famous canine was having his photograph taken again and again and again, as police queued up to have their picture taken with the Dog'.

The tourism complex at the site did an 'unprecedented trade in replicas of the Dog as thousands of travellers pulled in on Friday to see where the Dog wasn't'.

The 50th anniversary of the launching of the dog monument in 1982 inspired an article in the *Australian*, which included the following: '...the festivities will leave the resounding message that you wouldn't be Australian, you wouldn't be true blue, if the Dog on the Tuckerbox didn't mean something to you.'

And when the Melbourne *Age* tried to have a shot at 'another New South Wales institution', Dr Bernard Barrett, then state historian of Victoria, reminded it that the 'bolted canine was part of our heritage'.

This time Sir James Rowland, governor of New South Wales, unveiled the plaque, and the Howie Brothers released a record featuring their new song 'He's Been There For Fifty Years'. Improvements had been made to the site for the occasion.

When work on the new-look Hume Highway was

completed in 1984, the Dog monument ended up several hundred metres away. The old Hume Highway is now the access road to the tuckerbox complex.

Doggone! A toy blowup of the dog on the tuckerbox was installed with a notice ' Strayed to Canberra—back soon', when students stole the Dog for a Stone Day prank.

11 Gundagai—There's More than 'an Old-Fashioned Shack'

Fame must necessarily be the portion of but few.

R. Hall

Gundagai has a way of doing things that puts it in the limelight.

How many towns, or cities for that matter, have had songs written about them? Gundagai has had five— 'Along the Road to Gundagai', 'Where the Dog Sits on the Tuckerbox', 'Lazy Harry's', 'When the Boy from Alabama Meets the Girl from Gundagai' and 'Flash Jack from Gundagai'.

Where else is there a marble masterpiece of the brilliance of Rusconi's, with mind-boggling statistics attached to it? Commenced in 1910 and finished in 1938, it is on display at the Gundagai Tourist Centre, along with the artist's marble replica of the high altar in St Marie's Cathedral, just outside Paris.

Where else valuable photographs and original glass negatives of early twentieth century anywhere, as in the Gabriel collection of Gundagai?

Which other town can boast the most photographed attraction in Australia after Uluru, the Opera House and the Sydney Harbour Bridge? Despite the magnitude of these latter two edifices; despite the dog monument

Grace Power (nee Luff), the 1932 Tuckerbox Princess, with husband Art, cuts the 60th anniversary cake to the strains of 'Happy Birthday Dog'.

itself being unexceptional, and its history clouded; visitors are drawn to it from all over Australia.

And in 1992, when the Kansas City, Missouri, Parks and Gardens decided to add a feature of an overseas country to their zoo, and chose Australia, which town got the honour of having it named after it?

Why Gundagai of course!

Gundagai represents a history of a young nation that can be seen and felt. The legend of the Dog and the Tuckerbox has built for itself a spot in Australians' hearts second only to Waltzing Matilda.

The legend was started by a bullocky, reinforced by a poet, marketed by two newsagents, and above all, perpetuated by a songwriter.

The monument has been visited by English royalty in the form of the Duke of Gloucester in 1934, the Australian prime minister in 1932, the premier and governor of New South Wales in 1956 and 1982 respectively, to name but a few.

Although there will always be argument about its origins, and amusement that the monument to our pioneers was inspired by crude doggerel, nothing can diminish the place it has in history in making us aware of the conditions under which the early settlers lived, and their reliance on the bullockies to get supplies through to them.

Conroys Gap, which features in the first line of the original doggerel, is between Yass and Gundagai. It is described in *The Old Carrying Days* as 'another ugly rough piece of road that caused the teamsters trouble at times. On the Yass side there was an all too steep grade to negotiate, and on the opposite side the road was a rough rocky siding that called for very careful driving.'

The crossing of the Muttama Creek near Coolac was just one of the perils of the bullocky days, especially in winter. There wasn't always time to sit and wait for conditions to dry out the banks.

Many bullockies tried to make the crossing and paid the price—they got bogged. Some were hauled out by teamsters on the other side.

One lashed and swore and cried, but his Nobby strained and broke the yoke...and a legend was made when his dog sat in his tuckerbox, nine miles from Gundagai.

Index

Photograph Index